Published in the United S
Great Quotations Publishing
1967 Quincy Court
Glendale Heights, IL 60139

Printed in Hong Kong

D1458093

Phone Numbers

_____

_____

_____

_____

_____

_____

_____

_____

_____

_____

_____

_____

_____

_____

Quotes from Great Women

Special Occasions

_____

_____

_____

_____

_____

_____

_____

_____

_____

_____

_____

_____

_____

Every woman has a talent for greatness that is unique to that woman.

The truly great woman knows how to use her talents to impact not only the people around her, but the entire world.

Birthdays

Katharine Hepburn
Born 1906

This American actress is
known for her classic style
and witty charm.
Winner of both the
Emmy and Academy
Awards, she revealed
independence and strength
in her many film roles.

December 31

New Year's Eve

"What the New Year brings us will depend a great deal on what we bring to the New Year."

January 1

"Then sing, young hearts that are full of cheer,
With never a thought of sorrow;
The old goes out, but the glad young year
Comes merrily in tomorrow."

-Emily Miller

December 30

"We cannot make a new situation unless we are prepared to let go of what we hold most dear."

- Mary Caroline Richards

January 2

"*Without discipline,
there's no life at all.*"

- Katharine Hepburn

December 29

"No one is so eager to gain new experience
as he who doesn't know how to make use of
the old ones."

- Marie von Ebner-Eschenbach

January 3

" You never feel that you have fame.
It's always in back of you."

- Katharine Hepburn

December 28

"To follow, without hold, one aim:
That's the secret of success."

- Anna Pavlova

January 4

"It's life isn't it? You plow ahead and make a hit.
And you plow on and someone passes you.
Then someone passes them. Time levels."

— Katharine Hepburn

December 27

"Just don't give up trying to do what you really want to do. Where there's love and inspiration, I don't think you can go wrong."

- Ella Fitzgerald

January 5

"It is the plain women who know about love;
the beautiful women are too busy
being fascinating."

- Katharine Hepburn

December 26

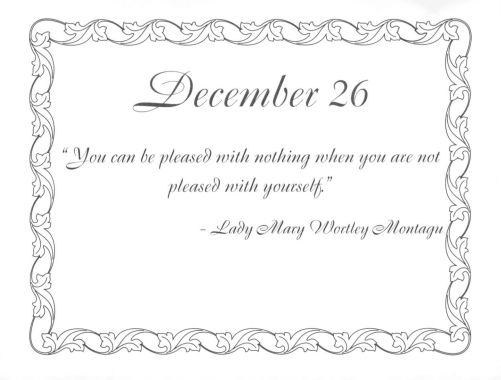

" You can be pleased with nothing when you are not pleased with yourself."

- Lady Mary Wortley Montagu

January 6

"If you obey all the rules
you miss all the fun."

-Katharine Hepburn

December 25

Christmas Day

"I do hope your Christmas has had a little touch of
Eternity in among the rush and pitter patter and all.
It always seems such a mixing of this world and
the next—but that after all is the idea!"

- Evelyn Underhill

January 7

"Character contributes to beauty. It fortifies a woman as her youth fades. A mode of conduct, a standard of courage, discipline, fortitude and integrity can do a great deal to make a woman beautiful."

-Jacqueline Bisset

December 24

"Christmas won't be Christmas
without any presents."

- Louisa May Alcott

January 8

"There are two ways of spreading light:
to be the candle or the mirror that receives it."

-Edith Wharton

December 23

"I can understand people simply fleeing the mountainous effort Christmas has become... But there are always a few saving graces and finally they make up for all the bother and distress."

- May Sarton

January 9

"*It's never to late too be what you might have been.*"

-George Eliot

December 22

"You have to learn the rules of the game.
And then you have to play better than
anyone else."

- Dianne Feinstein

January 10

"Fool!
Don't you see now that
I could have poisoned you a hundred times
had I been able to live without you!"

-Cleopatra to Marc Antony

December 21

The First Day of Winter

*"In a way winter is the real spring,
the time when the inner thing happens,
the resurge of nature."*

— Edna O'Brien

January 11

"It wasn't a woman who betrayed Jesus with a kiss."

-Catherine Carswell

December 20

"There's only one real sin,
and that is to persuade oneself that the
second-best is anything but the second-best."

- Doris Lessing

January 12

"*Elegance is innate...*
it has nothing to do
with being well dressed."

-Diana Vreeland

December 19

"Trouble is the common denominator of living. It is the great equalizer."

— Ann Landers

January 13

"The greatest happiness is
to transform one's feelings into actions..."

-Germaine de Staël

December 18

"I change myself, I change the world."

-Gloria Anzaldua

January 14

*"Love is the whole history
of a woman's life,
it is but an episode in a man's."*

-Germaine de Staël

December 17

"We fought hard. We gave it our best.
We did what was right.
And we made a difference."

- Geraldine Ferraro

January 15

The Birthday of Martin Luther King Jr.

"Non violence is...a spiritual discipline that requires a great deal of strength, growth, and purging of the self so that one can overcome almost any obstacle for the good of all without being concerned about one's own welfare."

- Coretta Scott King

December 16

"I think self-awareness is probably the most important thing towards being a champion."

- Billie Jean King

January 16

"A happy woman is one who has no cares at all;
a cheerful woman is one who has cares but doesn't
let them get her down."

-Beverly Sills

December 15

"I've always wanted to equalize things for us. ...Women can be great athletes. And I think we'll find in the next decade that women athletes will finally get the attention they deserve."

- Billie Jean King

January 17

"You may be disappointed if you fail,
but you are doomed if you don't try."

-Beverly Sills

December 14

"...women are carrying a new attitude.
They've cast aside the old stereotypes.
They don't believe you have to be ugly or have
big muscles to play sports."

- Shirley Johnson

January 18

"When something has been perfect...
there is a tendency to try hard to repeat it."

-Edna O'Brien

December 13

"...the most vital right is the right to love and be loved."

- Emma Goldman

January 19

"Success can make you go one of two ways. It can make you a prima donna, or it can smooth the edges, take away the insecurities, let the nice things come out."

-Barbara Walters

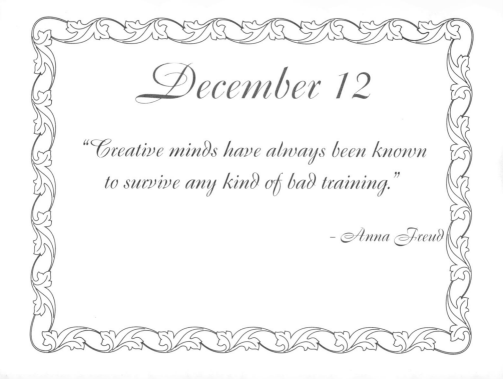

December 12

"Creative minds have always been known
to survive any kind of bad training."

- Anna Freud

January 20

"I believe in hard work.
It keeps the wrinkles out of the mind
and the spirit.
It helps to keep a woman young."

-Helena Rubenstein

December 11

"Think wrongly, if you please,
but in all cases think for yourself."

-Doris Lessing

January 21

"When people say: she's got everything,
I've only one answer:
I haven't had tomorrow."

-Elizabeth Taylor

December 10

"The trouble with most women is
they get old in their heads.
They think about it too much."

- Josephine Baker

January 22

*"I've never sought success
in order to get fame and money;
it's the talent and the passion
that count in success."*

-Ingrid Bergman

December 9

"If a man doesn't want a woman to express her own opinions and be funny, then he's not worth impressing."

-Carol Burnett

January 23

*"You cannot shake hands
with a clenched fist."*

-Indira Gandhi

December 8

"Everybody must learn this lesson somewhere - that it costs something to be what you are."

- Shirley Abbott

January 24

"*Don't compromise yourself.
You are all you've got.*"

—Betty Ford

December 7

"*Most women still need a room of their own and the only way to find it may be outside their own homes.*"

-Germaine Greer

January 25

"Let the world know you as you are,
not as you think you think you should be,
because sooner or later, if you are posing,
you will forget the pose, then where are you?"

-Fanny Brice

December 6

" *No vision and you perish;*
No ideal, and you're lost;
Your heart must ever cherish
Some faith at any cost."

- Harriet Du Autermont

January 26

"The way I see it,
if you want the rainbow,
you gotta put up with the rain."

-Dolly Parton

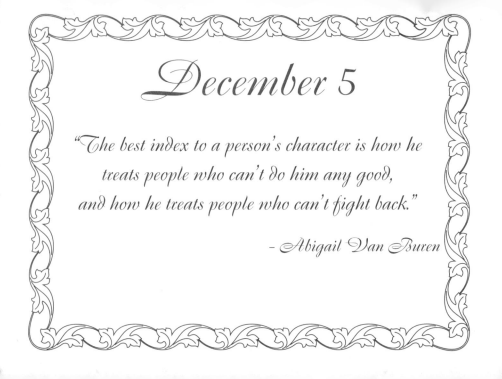

December 5

"The best index to a person's character is how he treats people who can't do him any good, and how he treats people who can't fight back."

- Abigail Van Buren

January 27

"People who fight fire with fire
usually end up with ashes."

— Abigail Van Buren

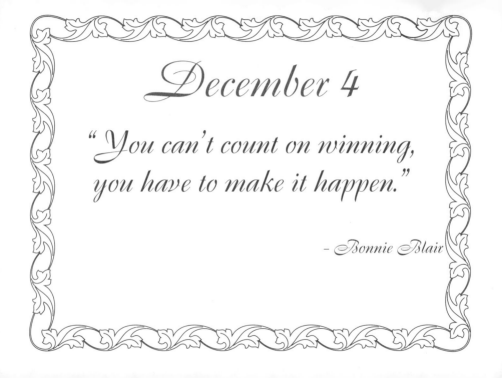

December 4

*" You can't count on winning,
you have to make it happen."*

- Bonnie Blair

January 28

"...that is what learning is .
You suddenly understand something
you've understood all your life,
but in a new way."

-Doris Lessing

December 3

"No matter what the competition, no matter what the training routine, I'd try to find a goal within it and try to better it."

— Bonnie Blair

January 29

*"Today the problem that has no name,
is how to juggle work,
love, home and children."*

- Betty Friedan

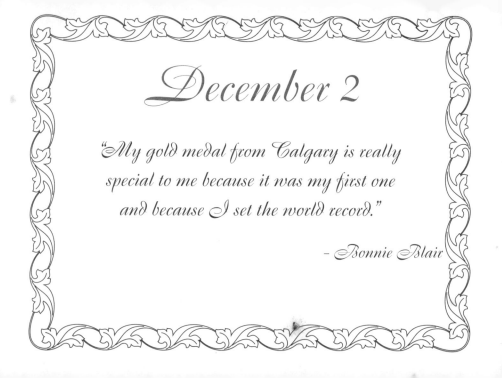

December 2

*"My gold medal from Calgary is really
special to me because it was my first one
and because I set the world record."*

– Bonnie Blair

January 30

"*Your heart often knows things before your mind does.*"

– Polly Adler

December 1

"Everyone was focusing on the rivalry - it's a great rivalry. But when I race, my focus is on myself and what I can do better."

- Bonnie Blair
(on her competition with China's Ye Qiaobo)

January 31

*"One man's way may be
as good as another's,
but we all like our own best."*

- Jane Austen

Bonnie Blair
Born 1964

The first US woman to win 3 Gold Medals in 3 different winter games, Bonnie made sport's history when she won her 4th Gold Medal in 1994. Her performances define grace under pressure.

Maya Angelou
Born 1928

A prolific novelist, poet,
playwright, short story
author, and performer.
Her series of
autobiographical works
describe the struggle
of a southern black woman
seeking physical
and spiritual liberation.

November 30

"This became a credo of mine...
attempt the impossible in order to
improve your work."

— Bette Davis

February 1

Black History Month

"Can you imagine if this country were not so afflicted with racism? Can you imagine what it would be like if the vitality, humor, and resilience of the black American were infused throughout this country?"

- Maya Angelou

November 29

"Can you imagine a world without men?
No crime and lots of happy fat women."

- (Sylvia) Nicole Hollander

February 2

*"The work, once completed, does not need me.
The work I'm working on needs my total
concentration. The one that's finished doesn't belong
to me anymore. It belongs to itself."*

- Maya Angelou

November 28

"To love what you do;
and feel that it matters –
how could anything be more fun?"

– Katherine Graham

February 3

"There's a world of difference
between truth and facts.
Facts can obscure the truth."

— Maya Angelou

November 27

"Motherhood and homemaking are honorable choices for any woman, provided it is the woman herself who makes those decisions."

- Molly Yard

February 4

"Love is like a virus.
It can happen to anybody at any
time."

- Maya Angelou

November 26

"Good health is more than just exercise and diet.
It is really a point of view and a mental attitude.
You can have the strongest body, but it's not good unless
the person inside of you has strength and optimism."

- Angela Lansbury

February 5

"Self-pity in its early stages is as snug as a feather mattress. Only when it hardens does it become uncomfortable."

- Maya Angelou

November 25

"I earn and pay my own way as a great many women do today. Why should unmarried women be discriminated against? Unmarried men are not."

- Dinah Shore

February 6

*"I note the obvious differences between each
sort and type, but we are more alike,
my friends,
than we are unalike."*

- Maya Angelou

November 24

*"Friends and good manners
will carry you where money won't go."*

- Margaret Walker

February 7

"Nobody, but nobody
Can make it out here alone."

- Maya Angelou

November 23

"The phrase working mother is redundant."

- Jane Sellman

February 8

"Children's talent to endure stems from their ignorance of alternatives."

- Maya Angelou

November 22

"Determination and perseverance move the world; thinking that others will do it for you is a sure way to fail."

– Marva Collins

February 9

"But what mother and daughter understand each other, or even have the sympathy for each other's lack of understanding?"

- Maya Angelou

November 21

*"...that is the best – to laugh with someone
because you both think the same things
are funny."*

- Gloria Vanderbilt

February 10

"I'm too young to be a legend.
I'm still the lady next door.
That keeps my feet on the ground."

- Aretha Franklin

November 20

"Trouble is a part of your life, and if you don't share it, you don't give the person who loves you enough chance to love you enough."

- Dinah Shore

February 11

"*Dignity is fighting weakness and winning.*"

— Lola Falana

November 19

"The man who treasures his friends
is usually solid gold himself."

- Marjorie Holmes

February 12

The Birthday of Abraham Lincoln

"I am convinced, the longer I live, that life & its blessings are not so entirely unjustly distribute as when we are suffering greatly, we are inclined to suppose – whilst others live on in a careless luke warm state – not appearing to fill Longfellow's measure: 'Into each life, some rain must fall.' "

- Mary Todd Lincoln

November 18

"A good woman inspires a man,
a brilliant woman interests him,
a beautiful woman fascinates him,
but a sympathetic woman gets him."

- Helen Rowland

February 13

"Soul is something creative, something active.
Soul is honesty. I sing to people about what matters.
I sing to the realists; people who accept it like it is.
I express problems, there are tears when it's sad and
smiles when it's happy. It seems simple to me, but to
some, feelings take courage."

- Aretha Franklin

November 17

"There is only one happiness in life,
to love and be loved..."

- George Sand

February 14
Saint Valentine's Day

*"Love understands love;
it needs no talk."*

— Frances Ridley Havergal

November 16

"*Where love is absent
there can be no woman.*"

- George Sand

February 15

"*When aroused,
the American conscience
is a powerful force for reform.*"

-Coretta Scott King

November 15

"The code of morality is to do unto others as you
would have them do unto you.
If you make that the central theme of your
morality code, it will serve you well
as a moral individual."

— Barbara Jordan

February 16

"Women, in general, are not a part of the corruption of the past, so they can give a new kind of leadership, a new image for mankind."

- Coretta Scott King

November 14

"I live a day at a time. Each day I look for a kernel of excitement. In the morning, I say: 'What is my exciting thing for today?' Then, I do the day. Don't ask me about tomorrow."

- Barbara Jordan

February 17

"I used to be very cold.
When you are cold you miss passion in your life.
I went for years just like ice.
I was killing myself. I was not loving back."

- Lena Horne

November 13

"...housewives, the natural people to turn to when there is something unpleasant, inconvenient or inconclusive to be done."

- Jane O'Reilly

February 18

"I didn't prepare myself to be seventy-one.
We should begin earlier to think about later on,
because we are all living longer."

- Lena Horne

November 12

"...the click! of recognition, that parenthesis of truth around a little thing that completes the puzzle of reality in women's minds – the moment that brings a gleam to our eyes and means the revolution has begun."

- Jane O'Reilly

February 19

*"Because time has been
good to me,
I treat it with great respect."*

— Lena Horne

November 11

"*I dream and plan as if there was nothing happening in the world, as if there was no war, no destruction.*"

- Hannah Senesh

February 20

"You can't get too high for somebody to bring you down."

- Billie Holiday

November 10

"To have a reason to get up in the morning, it is necessary to possess a guiding principle.
A belief of some kind.
A bumper sticker if you will."

- Judith Guest

February 21

"Sometimes it's worse to win a fight than to lose."

- Billie Holiday

November 9

"All women hustle. Women watch faces, voices, gestures, moods. The person who has to survive through cunning."

- Marge Piercy

February 22

The Birthday of George Washington

" ...the greater part of our happiness or misery depends on our
dispositions, and not on our circumstances. We carry the
seeds of the one or the other about with us in our minds
wherever we go."

- Martha Washington

November 8

"I refuse to believe that trading recipes is silly.
Tuna-fish casserole is at least as real
as corporate stock."

- Barbara Grizzuti Harrison

February 23

"If you set out to be successful,
then you already are."

– Katherine Dunham

November 7

"Women's propensity to share confidences is universal. We confirm our reality by sharing."

- Barbara Grizzuti Harrison

February 24

"It's easy to be independent when you've got money.
But to be independent when you haven't got a
thing - that's the Lord's test."

- Mahalia Jackson

November 6

"We all live with the objective of being happy; our lives are all different and yet the same."

- Anne Frank

February 25

"*If you don't look out for others, who will look out for you?*"

— Whoopi Goldberg

November 5

"Parents can only give good advice or put them on the right paths, but the final forming of a person's character lies in their own hands."

- Anne Frank

February 26

*"Whatever I'm doing,
I don't think in terms of tomorrow."*

- Anita Baker

November 4

"Think of all the beauty still left around you and be happy."

– Anne Frank

February 27

*"You leave home to seek your fortune
and when you get it you go home
and share it with your family."*

- Anita Baker

November 3

*"How wonderful it is that nobody
need wait a single moment before starting
to improve the world."*

- Anne Frank

February 28

"*We will build a democratic America in spite of undemocratic Americans.*
We have rarely worried about the odds or the obstacles before – we will not start worrying now.
We will have both of our goals – Peace and Power!

– Shirley Chisholm

November 2

*"Laziness may appear attractive,
but work gives satisfaction."*

- Anne Frank

February 29

*"To live is to suffer;
to survive is to find some meaning in
the suffering."*

- Roberta Flack

November 1

"*Whoever is happy will make others happy too.*
He who has courage and faith will
never perish in misery!"

- *Anne Frank*

Sandra Day O'Connor
Born 1930

A mother of 3 sons and at one time a full-time housewife, this graduate of Stanford University went on to become the first woman judge of the United States Supreme Court.

Anne Frank
1929–1945

In a small diary Anne recorded poetry and stories, along with her hopes, fears, and reflections during the two years she and her family were hiding from Nazi persecution. She died in a prison camp at the age of 16.

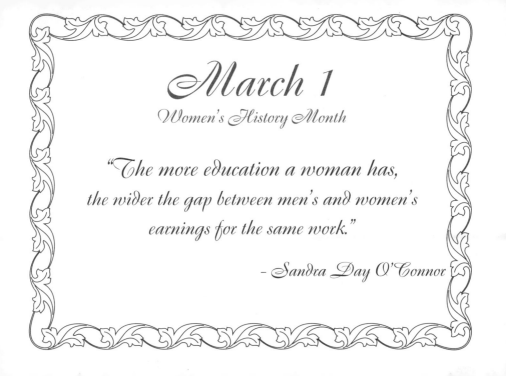

March 1

Women's History Month

*"The more education a woman has,
the wider the gap between men's and women's
earnings for the same work."*

- Sandra Day O'Connor

October 31

Halloween

"A witch was a woman with enormous power,
a woman who might change the natural world.
She was uncivilized and in opposition to the world of the
King, the court, polite society. She had to be controlled."

- Louise Bernikow

March 2

"*Despite the encouraging and wonderful gains and the changes for women which have occurred in my lifetime, there is still room to advance and to promote correction of the remaining deficiencies and imbalances.*"

- Sandra Day O'Connor

October 30

"*And the trouble is,
if you don't risk anything,
you risk even more.*"

— *Erica Jong*

March 3

"When people are more successful than they had imagined, nothing is ever achieved without giving something up."

-Judith M. Bardwick

October 29

"*You can take no credit for beauty at 16.
But if you are beautiful at 60,
it will be your own soul's doing.*"

- Marie Stopes

March 4

"Being powerful is like being a lady. If you have to tell people you are, you aren't."

- Margaret Thatcher

October 28

"We ought to be able to learn some things second hand. There is not enough time for us to make all the mistakes ourselves."

- Harriet Hall

March 5

"No one would remember the Good Samaritan
if he'd only had good intentions.
He had money as well."

- Margaret Thatcher

October 27

"Failure is a luxury not yet afforded to women."

– Susan Seidelman

March 6

*"I am extraordinarily patient,
provided I get my own way in the end."*

- Margaret Thatcher

October 26

"*Even when you plan to have a family, you never know who the person is going to be that you decide to become a parent to. We're accidentally born to our own parents.*"

- Louise Erdrich

March 7

"*No one can make you feel inferior without your consent.*"

– Eleanor Roosevelt

October 25

"What of October, that ambiguous month, the month of tension, the unendurable month?"

- Doris Lessing

March 8

" You have to accept whatever comes and the only important thing is that you meet it with courage and with the best you have to give."

- Eleanor Roosevelt

October 24

"*Women of the world, united without any regard for national or racial divisions, become a most powerful force for international peace.*"

-Coretta Scott King

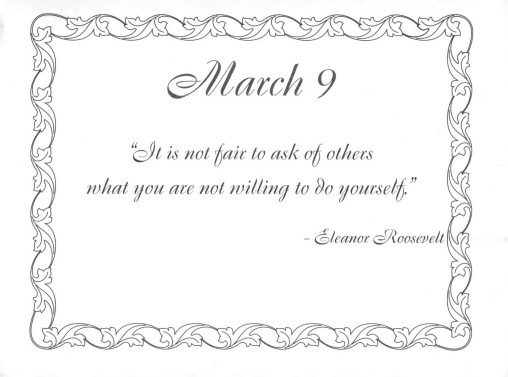

March 9

*"It is not fair to ask of others
what you are not willing to do yourself."*

- Eleanor Roosevelt

October 23

*"Man forgives woman anything
save the wit to outwit him."*

- Minna Antrim

March 10

"I gain strength, courage and confidence by every experience in which I must stop and look fear in the face ... I say to myself, I've lived through this and can take the next thing that comes along... We must do the things we think we cannot do."

- Eleanor Roosevelt

October 22

*"Everyone has talent. What is rare is the
courage to follow the talent to the dark place
where it leads."*

- Lucy Stone

March 11

The purpose of life, after all, is to live it,
to taste experience to the utmost,
to reach out eagerly and without fear
for newer and richer experiences.

- Eleanor Roosevelt

October 21

"I don't think success is harmful,
as so many people say.
Rather, I believe it indispensable to talent,
if for nothing else than to increase the talent."

- Jeanne Moreau

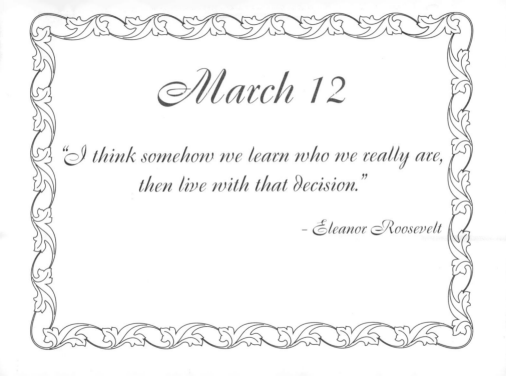

March 12

*"I think somehow we learn who we really are,
then live with that decision."*

- Eleanor Roosevelt

October 20

*"Dwelling on the negative
simply contributes to its power."*

- Shirley MacLaine

March 13

"Far away there in the sunshine are my
highest aspirations. I may not reach them,
but I can look up and see their beauty, believe in
them and try to follow where they lead."

– Louisa May Alcott

October 19

"Maybe the tragedy of the human race was that we had forgotten we were each Divine."

- Shirley MacLaine

March 14

"Fame is a pearl many dive for and only a few
bring up. Even when they do,
it is not perfect, and they sigh for more,
and lose better things in struggling for them."

- Louisa May Alcott

October 18

"Nothing should be permanent except struggle with the dark side within ourselves."

- Shirley MacLaine

March 15

"I'm not afraid of storms,
for I'm learning how to sail my ship."

- Louisa May Alcott

October 17

"The older I get,
the more of my mother
I see in myself."

- Nancy Friday

March 16

- Four Leaf Clover -
One leaf is for hope, and one is for faith,
And one is for love, you know,
And God put another in for luck.

- Ella Higginson

October 16

*"To gain that which is worth having,
it may be necessary to lose everything else."*

- Bernadette Devlin

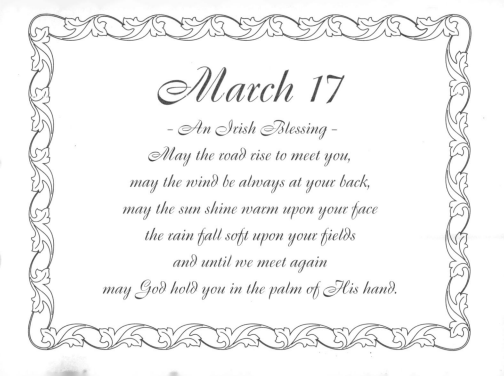

March 17

- An Irish Blessing -

May the road rise to meet you,

may the wind be always at your back,

may the sun shine warm upon your face

the rain fall soft upon your fields

and until we meet again

may God hold you in the palm of His hand.

October 15

"Any woman who chooses to behave like a full human being should be warned that armies of the status quo will treat her as something of a dirty joke; that's their natural and first weapon."

-Gloria Steinem

March 18

"...love is the only thing that we can
carry with us when we go,
and it makes the end so easy."

- Louisa May Alcott

October 14

"The Golden Rule works for men as written,
but for women it should go the other way around.
We need to do unto ourselves as we do unto others."

- Gloria Steinem

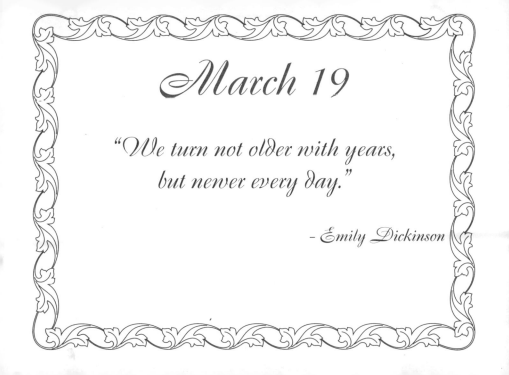

March 19

"We turn not older with years,
but newer every day."

- Emily Dickinson

October 13

"The first problem for all of us, men and women, is not to learn but to unlearn."

-Gloria Steinem

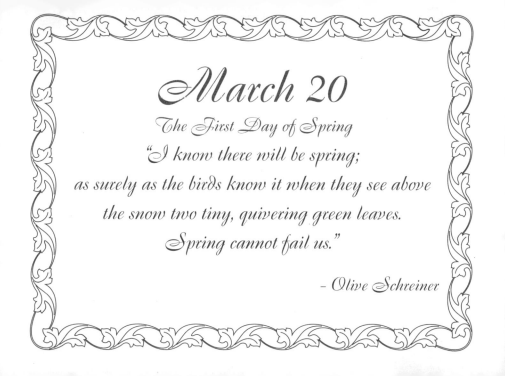

March 20

The First Day of Spring

"I know there will be spring;
as surely as the birds know it when they see above
the snow two tiny, quivering green leaves.
Spring cannot fail us."

- Olive Schreiner

October 12

Columbus Day

"Columbus only discovered that he was in some new place. He didn't discover America."

- Louise Erdrich

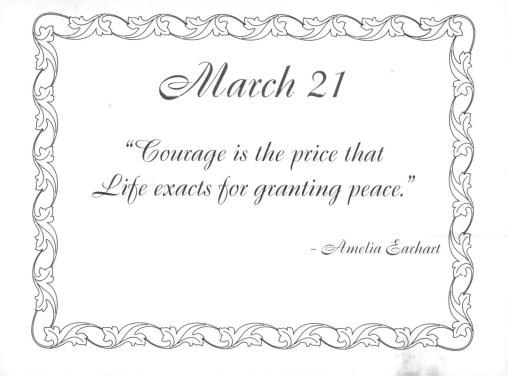

March 21

"*Courage is the price that
Life exacts for granting peace.*"

- Amelia Earhart

October 11

*"I have found the paradox that if I love
until it hurts, then there is no hurt,
but only more love."*

- Mother Teresa

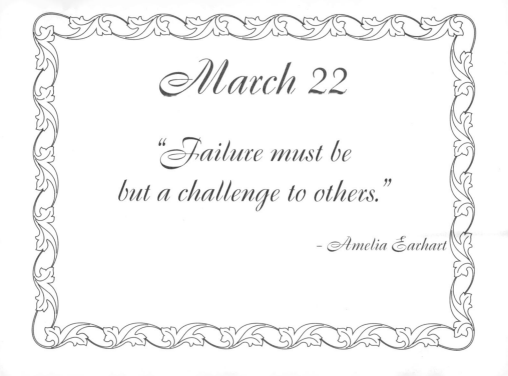

March 22

"*Failure must be
but a challenge to others.*"

— Amelia Earhart

October 10

"Kind words can be short and easy to speak,
but their echoes are truly endless."

- Mother Teresa

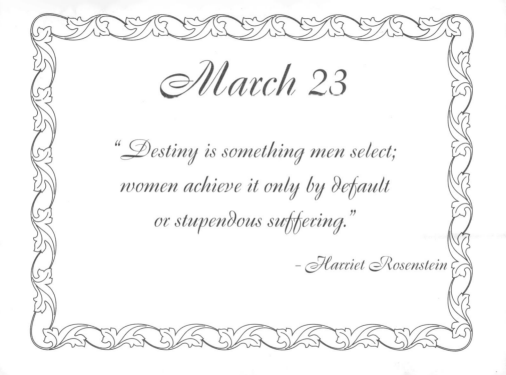

March 23

"*Destiny is something men select;
women achieve it only by default
or stupendous suffering.*"

- Harriet Rosenstein

October 9

"*Joy is a net of love by which you can catch souls.*"

– Mother Teresa

March 24

"*I never notice what has been done.*
I only see what remains to be done."

- Madam Curie

October 8

*"To keep a lamp burning
we have to keep putting oil in it."*

- Mother Teresa

March 25

"I have to really feel a song before I'll deal with it and just about every song I do is based either on an experience I've had or an experience someone I knew had gone through."

- Aretha Franklin

October 7

*"It is by forgiving
that one is forgiven."*

— Mother Teresa

March 26

*"Ambition if it feeds at all,
does so on the ambition of others."*

- Susan Sontag

October 6

"Never bend your head. Always hold it high. Look the world straight in the eye."

- Helen Keller

March 27

...old age is like a plane flying through a storm. Once you're aboard, there's nothing you can do. You can't stop the plane, you can't stop the storm, you can't stop time. So one might as well accept it calmly, wisely.

- Golda Meir

October 5

"*Life is either a daring adventure or nothing.*
To keep our faces toward change
and behave like free spirits in the presence of fate is
strength undefeatable."

- Helen Keller

March 28

"*I must govern the clock,
not be governed by it.*"

-Golda Meir

October 4

"*No pessimist ever discovered the secrets of the stars,
or sailed to an uncharted land,
or opened a new heaven to the human spirit.*"

– Helen Keller

March 29

"At work, you think of the children you have left at home. At home, you think of the work you've left unfinished. Such a struggle is unleashed within yourself. Your heart is rent."

—Golda Meir

October 3

"*Many persons have a wrong idea of what constitutes real happiness. It is not obtained through self-gratification, but through fidelity to a worthy purpose.*"

- Helen Keller

March 30

"To be successful,
a woman has to be better at her job
than a man."

— Golda Meir

October 2

"When we do the best that we can, we never know
what miracle is wrought in our life,
or in the life of another."

- Helen Keller

March 31

"Those who do not know how to
weep with their whole heart
don't know how to laugh either."

- Golda Meir

October 1

"Character cannot be developed in ease and quiet. Only through experience of trial and suffering can the soul be strengthened, vision cleared, ambition inspired, and success achieved."

- Helen Keller

Bette Midler
Born 1945

*Recognized
throughout the world for
her brazen wit, satirical
humor and camp
performance style,
this singer/actress has won
both Emmy and
Grammy awards.*

Helen Keller
1880–1968

Helen Keller's world
was dark and
silent until her friend and
teacher Anne Sullivan
helped her learn to read,
speak, and write. Ms.
Keller spent her adult life
bettering the
conditions of others.

April 1

National Humor Month

"A good laugh is good for the spirits it's true,
But a good cry is good for the soul."

- Bette Midler

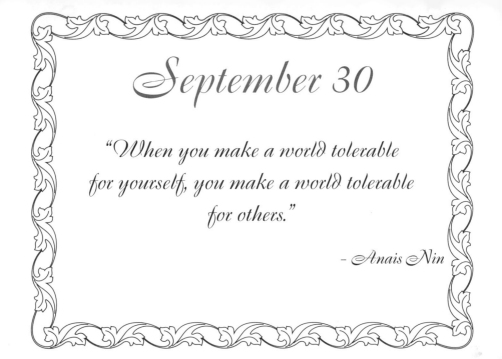

September 30

"When you make a world tolerable for yourself, you make a world tolerable for others."

- Anais Nin

April 2

"I always try to balance the light with the heavy - a few tears for the human spirit in with the sequins and the fringes."

— Bette Midler

September 29

"Dreams pass into the reality of action. From the action stems the dream again; and this interdependence produces the highest form of living."

— Anais Nin

April 3

"After thirty,
a body has a mind of its own."

- Bette Midler

September 28

"*Life shrinks or expands
in proportion to one's courage.*"

— Anais Nin

April 4

"Make sure that your life is a rare entertainment! It doesn't take anything drastic. You needn't be gorgeous or wealthy or smart. Just very enthusiastic!"

– Bette Midler

September 27

"What I cannot love, I overlook.
Is that real friendship?"

- Anais Nin

April 5

*"Marriage involves big compromises all the time.
International-level compromises.
You're the USA, he's the USSR,
and you're talking nuclear warheads."*

- Bette Midler

September 26

*"I don't do anything wrong,
I'm perfect."*

- Bonnie Domingo

April 6

"The trouble with the rat race is
that even if you win,
you're still a rat."

- Lily Tomlin

September 25

"Woman's work!
House work's the hardest work in the world.
That's why men won't do it."

- Edna Ferber

April 7

"If you can't be direct, why be?"

— Lily Tomlin

September 24

"Where should one use perfume?"
a young woman asked.
"Wherever one wants to be kissed," I said.

-Coco Chanel

April 8

"*Most mothers are instinctive philosophers.*"

-Harriet Beecher Stowe

September 23

The First Day of Autumn

"*Delicious autumn! My very soul is wedded to it, and if I were a bird I would fly about the earth seeking the successive autumns.*"

-George Eliot

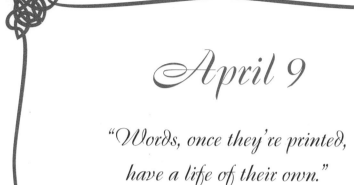

April 9

"Words, once they're printed,
have a life of their own."

- Carol Burnett

September 22

"There are sounds to seasons.
There are sounds to places, and there are sounds
to every time in one's life."

- Alison Wyrley Birch

April 10

"The suburbs were discovered, quite by accident,
one day in the early 1940s by a
Welcome Wagon lady who was lost."

- Erma Bombeck

September 21

I have always felt that a woman has the right to treat the subject of her age with ambiguity until, perhaps, she passes into the realm of over ninety. Then it is better she be candid with herself and with the world.

- Helena Rubinstein

April 11

"It seemed rather incongruous that in a society of
supersophisticated communication,
we often suffer from a shortage of listeners."

- Erma Bombeck

September 20

"To a woman, the consciousness of being well-dressed gives a sense of tranquility which religion fails to bestow."

- Helen Olcott Bell

April 12

*"Superior people
never make very long visits."*

– Marianne Moore

September 19

"Opportunities are usually
disguised by hard work,
so most people don't recognize them."

- Ann Landers

April 13

"From birth to age 18, a girl needs good parents,
from 18 to 35 she needs good looks,
from 35 to 55 she needs a good personality,
and from 55 on she needs cash."

- Sophie Tucker

September 18

"If I have to, I can do anything.
I am strong, I am invincible,
I am Woman."

- Helen Reddy

April 14

"Being a funny person does an awful lot of things to you.
You feel that you mustn't get serious with people.
They don't expect it from you, and they don't want to see it.
You're not entitled to be serious, you're a clown,
and they only want you to make them laugh."

- Fanny Brice

September 17

"Glamour to me is being
spotlessly clean
and courteous at all times."

— Helen Reddy

April 15

"Comedy is very controlling - you are making people laugh. It is there in the phrase 'making people laugh'. You feel completely in control when you hear a wave of laughter coming back at you that you have caused."

-Gilda Radner

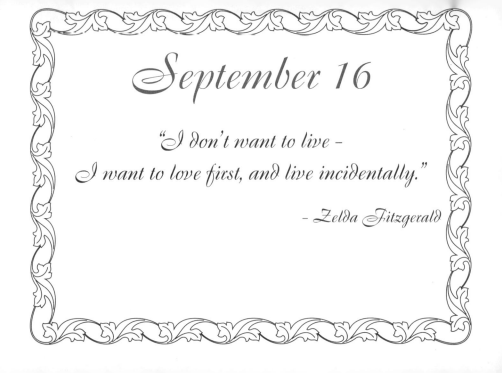

September 16

"I don't want to live –
I want to love first, and live incidentally."

- Zelda Fitzgerald

April 16

"I'd much rather be a woman than a man. Women can cry, they can wear cute clothes, and they're first to be rescued off sinking ships."

- Gilda Radner

September 15

"Protocol is not there to dictate to you.
It's there to help you. You have to have the
courage and security to do it your way."

- Barbara Bush

April 17

"I've always thought women
were much more dangerous than men."

- Tina Howe

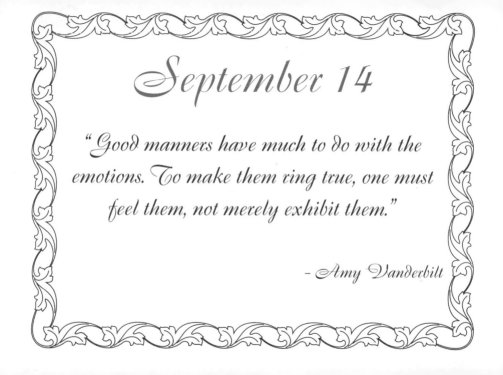

September 14

"Good manners have much to do with the emotions. To make them ring true, one must feel them, not merely exhibit them."

- Amy Vanderbilt

April 18

"The best way to hold a man
is in your arms."

- Mae West

September 13

"I come from people who have always been polite enough to feel that nothing has ever happened to them."

- Patricia Hampl

April 19

"Men have structured society to make a woman feel guilty if she looks after herself. Well, I beat men at their own game. I don't look down on men but I certainly don't look up to them either. I never found a man I could love - or trust - the way I loved myself."

- Mae West

September 12

"Civility costs nothing,
and buys everything."

– Lady Mary Wortley Montagu

April 20

"One can never be too thin
or too rich."

- Wallis Simpson Windsor

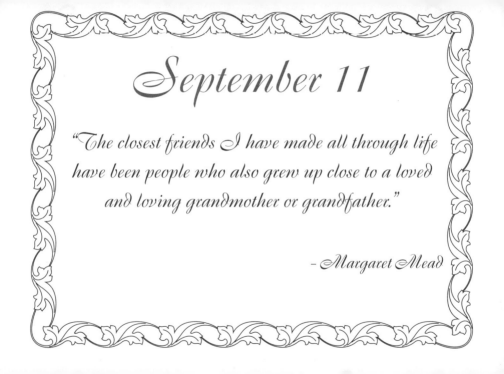

September 11

"The closest friends I have made all through life have been people who also grew up close to a loved and loving grandmother or grandfather."

- Margaret Mead

April 21

*"Now sometimes it can be a very dangerous
thing to go in search of a dream
for the reality does not always match it..."*

- Gracie Fields

September 10

"It is not rude to turn off your telephone by switching it on to an answering machine, which is cheaper and less disruptive than ripping it out of the wall. Those who are offended because they cannot always get through when they seek, at their own convenience, to barge in on people are suffering from a rude expectation."

- Judith Martin

April 22

"Loving a child doesn't mean giving in to all his whims; to love him is to bring out the best in him, to teach him to love what is difficult."

- Nadia Boulanger

September 9

"The dinner table is the center for the teaching and practicing not just of table manners but of conversation, consideration, tolerance, family feeling, and just about all the other accomplishment of polite society except the minuet."

– Judith Martin

April 23

"They should have hired me when I was
eighteen and knew everything...
I'd be the boss by now."

- Laura Mauk

September 8

*"Ideological differences
are no excuse for rudeness."*

— Judith Martin

April 24

"If you see the magic in a fairy tale,
you can face the future."

- Danielle Steel

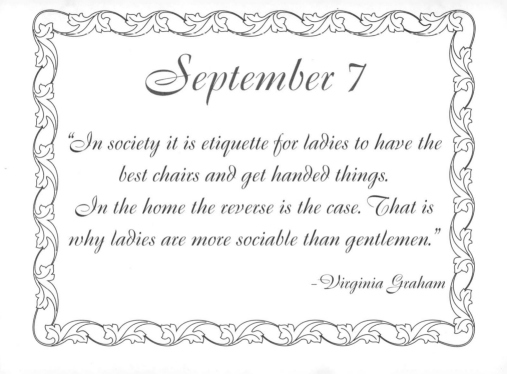

September 7

"In society it is etiquette for ladies to have the
best chairs and get handed things.
In the home the reverse is the case. That is
why ladies are more sociable than gentlemen."

-Virginia Graham

April 25

"It is almost impossible to throw dirt on someone without getting a little on yourself."

- Abigail Van Buren

September 6

Every great mistake has a halfway moment,
a split second when it can be recalled
and perhaps remedied.

- Pearl S. Buck

April 26

"We all have the same dreams."

- Joan Didion

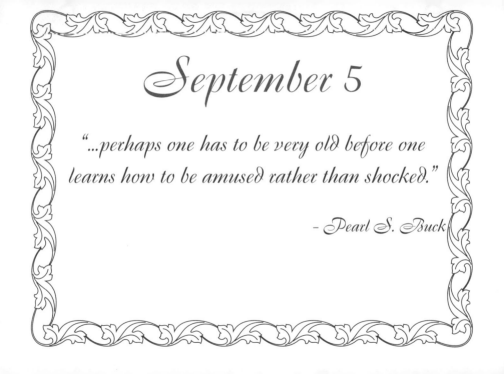

September 5

"...perhaps one has to be very old before one learns how to be amused rather than shocked."

- Pearl S. Buck

April 27

"The average secretary in the U.S. is better educated than the average boss."

- Gloria Steinem

September 4

" *You cannot make yourself feel something you do not feel, but you can make yourself do right in spite of your feelings.*"

— Pearl S. Buck

April 28

"To be successful, the first thing to do is fall in love with your work."

- Sister Mary Lauretta

September 3

"I feel no need for any other faith than my faith in human beings."

- Pearl S. Buck

April 29

"Luck? I don't know anything about luck.
I've never banked on it, and I'm afraid of people
who do. Luck to me is something else:
Hard work - and realizing what is
opportunity and what isn't."

- Lucille Ball

September 2

"The secret of joy in work is contained in one word -excellence. To know how to do something well is to enjoy it."

- Pearl S. Buck

April 30

*"I think knowing what you can not do is more
important than knowing what you can do.
In fact, that's good taste."*

- Lucille Ball

September 1

"All things are possible until they are proved impossible – and even the impossible may only be so as of now."

– Pearl S. Buck

Anne Morrow Lindbergh
Born 1906

The wife of avaitor Charles Lindbergh, she accompanied him as copilot, navigator, and photographer. After the tragic kidnapping of their first son, Mrs. Lindbergh raised 5 children and continued to write her inspiring books.

Pearl S. Buck
1892–1973

Through her novels, which centered around Chinese life, she hoped to make the East, its ways, and its people more understandable to Westerners. She received both a Pulitzer Prize and a Nobel Prize for literature.

May 1

"Only in growth, reform, and change,
paradoxically enough,
is true security to be found."

\- Anne Morrow Lindbergh

August 31

*"Integrity is so perishable
in the summer months of success."*

-Vanessa Redgrave

May 2

"Too many people, too many demands,
too much to do; competent, busy,
hurrying people – It just isn't living at all."

- Anne Morrow Lindbergh

August 30

"There is no substitute
for hard work."

- Florence Griffith Joyner

May 3

"Total freedom is never what one imagines and, in fact, hardly exists. It comes as a shock in life to learn that we usually only exchange one set of restrictions for another. The second set, however, is self-chosen, and therefore easier to accept."

- Anne Morrow Lindbergh

August 29

*"All my life through,
the new sights of nature made me
rejoice like a child."*

— Madam Curie

May 4

*"If you let yourself be absorbed completely,
if you surrender completely to the moments as they
pass, you live more richly those moments."*

- Anne Morrow Lindbergh

August 28

"Nothing in life is to be feared.
It is only to be understood."

- Madame Curie

May 5

"By and large, mothers and housewives are the only
workers who do not have regular time off.
They are the great vacationless class."

- Anne Morrow Lindbergh

August 27

"It is easier to live through someone else than to become complete yourself."

- Betty Friedan

May 6

"Women never have a half-hour in all their lives (excepting before or after anybody is up in the house) that they can call their own, without fear of offending or of hurting someone. Why do people sit up so late, or, more rarely, get up so early? Not because the day is not long enough, but because they have no time in the day to themselves.

- Florence Nightingale

August 26

"I have always felt that the moment when first you wake up in the morning is the most wonderful of the twenty-four hours. No matter how weary or dreary you may feel, you possess the certainty that...absolutely anything may happen. And the fact that it practically always doesn't, matters not one jot. The possibility is always there."

- Monica Baldwin

May 7

"There's a period of life when we swallow
a knowledge of ourselves and it becomes
either good or sour inside."

- Pearl Bailey

August 25

"Perhaps the straight and narrow path would be wider if more people used it."

— Kay Ingram

May 8

"You never get over being a child,
long as you have a mother to go to."

- Sarah Orne Jewett

August 24

*"The moon develops the imagination,
as chemicals develop photographic images."*

- Sheila Ballantyne

May 9

"The rare and beautiful experiences of divine revelation are moments of special gifts. Each of us, however, lives each day with special gifts which are a part of our very being, and life is a process of discovering and developing these God-given gifts within each of us."

– Jeanne Dixon

August 23

"The best way to attract money,
she had discovered,
was to give the appearance of having it."

-Gail Sheehy

May 10

*"Blessed are those who can give
without remembering,
and take without forgetting."*

- Elizabeth Bibesco

August 22

"Who can tell the range of joy
Or set the bounds of beauty?"

- Sara Teasdale

May 11

"This is something that I cherish.

Once in a friend's home I came across this blessing, and took it

down in shorthand...it says something I like to live with:

"Oh Thou, who dwellest in so many homes, possess Thyself of

this. Bless the life that is sheltered here. Grant that trust and

peace and comfort abide within, and that love and life and use-

fulness may go out from this home forever."

-Claudia ("Lady Bird") Johnson

August 21

"I paint from the top down.
First the sky, then the mountains, then the hills,
then the houses, then the cattle,
and then the people."

-Grandma Moses

May 12

"Make sure you never, never argue at night. You just lose a good night's sleep, and you can't settle anything until morning anyway."

- Rose Fitzgerald Kennedy

August 20

"What a strange thing is memory, and hope;
one looks backward, the other forward.
The one is of today, the other is of tomorrow.
Memory is history recorded in our brain, memory is a
painter, it paints pictures of the past and of the day."

-Grandma Moses

May 13

"Birds sing after a storm;
why shouldn't people feel as free to delight
in whatever remains to them?"

— Rose Fitzgerald Kennedy

August 19

"If I didn't start painting,
I would have raised chickens."

– Grandma Moses

May 14

*"Sedentary people are apt to have sluggish minds.
A sluggish mind is apt to be reflected in
flabbiness of body and in a dullness of expression
that invites no interest and gets none."*

– Rose Fitzgerald Kennedy

August 18

"I look back on my life like a good day's work, it was done and I am satisfied with it."

-Grandma Moses

May 15

"The test for whether or not you can hold a job
should not be the arrangement
of your chromosomes."

- Bella Abzug

August 17

"I am never free of the past. I have made it crystal clear that I believe the past is part of the present which becomes part of the future."

- Lee Krasner

May 16

*"Men their rights and nothing more;
women their rights and nothing less."*

- Susan B. Anthony

August 16

"In the end, what affects your life
most deeply are things too simple
to talk about."

— Nell Blaine

May 17

"If one is rich and one's a woman,
one can be quite misunderstood."

- Katharine Graham

August 15

"*Art is the signature of civilizations.*"

— Beverly Sills

May 18

*"The history of every country begins in
the heart of a man or woman."*

- Willa Cather

August 14

"After the verb 'To Love',
"To Help' is the most beautiful verb
in the world!"

- Bertha von Suttner

May 19

"Why can't we build orphanages next to homes
for the elderly? If someone's sitting
in a rocker, it won't be long before a kid will
be in his lap."

-Cloris Leachman

August 13

"True strength is delicate."

- Louise Nevelson

May 20

"Brevity may be the soul of wit,
but not when someone's saying, 'I love you.'"

- Judith Viorst

August 12

"I like living. I have sometimes been wildly, despairingly, acutely miserable, racked with sorrow, but through it all I still know quite certainly that just to be alive is a grand thing."

- Agatha Christie

May 21
Armed Forces Day

"If peace, he thought
(as he had often thought before),
only had the music and pageantry of war, there'd be
no more wars."

- Sophie Kerr

August 11

"The test of a man is how well he is able to feel about what he thinks. The test of a woman is how well she is able to think about what she feels."

– Mary S. McDowell

May 22

"Every time I think that I'm getting old, and gradually going to the grave, something else happens."

- Lillian Carter

August 10

"It is not easy to find happiness in ourselves, and
impossible to find it elsewhere."

– Agnes Repplier

May 23

"...women are the real architects of society."

- Harriet Beecher Stowe

August 9

"All art requires courage."

– Anne Tucker

May 24

"When you get into a tight place and everything goes against you, till it seems as though you could not hang on a minute longer, never give up then, for that is just the place and time that the tide will turn."

- Harriet Beecher Stowe

August 8

"Life engenders life. Energy creates energy.
It is by spending oneself that one
becomes rich."

- Sarah Bernhardt

May 25

*"You will do foolish things,
but do them with enthusiasm."*

– Colette

August 7

"You don't get to choose how you're going to die. Or when. You can only decide how you're going to live. Now."

– Joan Baez

May 26

"But I suppose experience of life
will in time teach you that tact is a very
essential ingredient in all things."

- Jennie Jerome Churchill

August 6

"Where I was born and where and how
I have lived is unimportant. It is what
I have done with where I have been that
should be of interest."

-Georgia O'Keefe

May 27

"It is delightful to be a woman;
but every man thanks the Lord devoutly
that he isn't one."

– Olive Schreiner

August 5

"I feel there is something unexplored about women that only a woman can explore..."

-Georgia O'Keefe

May 28

"I am more and more convinced
that man is a dangerous creature."

- Abigail Adams

August 4

"I believe that to create one's own world in any of the arts takes courage."

- Georgia O'Keefe

May 29

"Please know that I am aware of the hazards.
I want to do it because I want to do it.
Women must try to do things as men have tried.
When they fail, their failure must be but a
challenge to others."

- Amelia Earhart

August 3

"The first feeling was hunger for reality and sincerity, a desire for simplicity."

- Georgia O'Keefe

May 30
Memorial Day

"From Memorial Day to Labor Day,
you may wear white shoes. Not before and not after.
As a command, the White Shoe Edict should be clear
and simple enough. Do not violate it."

-Judith Martin

August 2

"Nobody sees a flower - really - it is so small - we haven't the time - and to see takes time like to have a friend takes time."

- Georgia O'Keefe

May 31

*"You take people as far as they will go,
not as far as you would like them to go."*

- Jeannette Rankin

August 1

American Artist's Appreciation Month

"*I want real things –
music that makes holes in the sky.*"

- Georgia O'Keefe

Sally Kirsten Ride
Born 1951

Her mission aboard the shuttle Challenger, secured her place in history as the first United States woman in space. She could have been a professional tennis player but instead chose to pursue astrophysics.

Georgia O'Keefe
Born 1887

Best known for her large,
semi-abstract studies of
flowers and sun-dried
bones. She was married
to photographer
Alfred Stieglitz,
and was one
of his favorite subjects.

June 1

Cat Month

"I did not come to NASA to make history - it is important to me that people don't think I was picked for the flight because I am a woman and it's time for NASA to send one."

- Sally Ride

July 31

"*Housework is the hardest work in the world.*
That's why men won't do it."

-Edna Ferber

June 2

"You spend a year training just which dials to look at and when the time comes, all you want to do is look out the window. It's so beautiful."

- Sally Ride

July 30

"There is nothing enduring
in the life of a woman
except what she builds in a man's heart."

- Judith Anderson

June 3

*"I'm sure it's the most fun
I'll ever have in my life."*

- Sally Ride

July 29

"The thing women have got to learn is that nobody gives you power. You just take it."

- Roseanne Barr Arnold

June 4

"It is better, under certain circumstances,
to be a cat than to be a duchess ...
no duchess of the realm ever had more faithful
retainers or half so abject subjects."

- Helen M. Winslow

July 28

"I think the one lesson I have learned is that there is no substitute for paying attention."

-Diane Sawyer

June 5

"My cat does not talk as respectfully
to me as I do to her."

—Colette

July 27

"A man has to be Joe McCarthy
to be called ruthless.
All a woman has to do is put you on hold."

- Marlo Thomas

June 6

"*Animals are such agreeable friends,
they ask no questions,
they pass no criticisms.*"

— George Eliot

July 26

*"My feeling is that there is nothing in life
but refraining from hurting others,
and comforting those that are sad."*

- Olive Schreiner

June 7

"Is it enough to know that one creature likes
what you do and the way you do it
and that creature is your cat?"

— Naomi Thornton

July 25

"I am never afraid of what I know."

- Anna Sewell

June 8

"What are we doing here?
We're reaching for the stars."

—Christa McAuliffe

July 24

*"One of the things about equality is
not just that you be treated equally to a man,
but that you treat yourself equally
to the way you treat a man."*

— Marlo Thomas

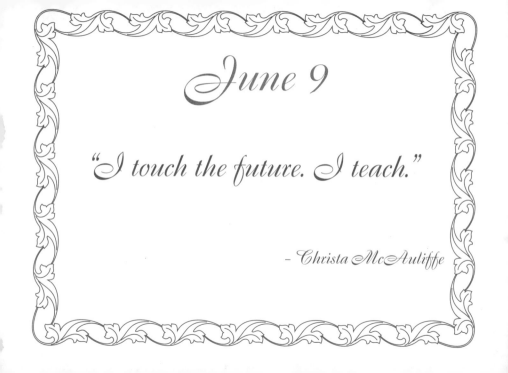

June 9

"I touch the future. I teach."

— Christa McAuliffe

July 23

"*Reality is something you rise above.*"

- *Liza Minelli*

June 10

"I was not looking for my dreams to interpret my life, but rather for my life to interpret my dreams."

- Susan Sontag

July 22

"You can't be brave if you've only had wonderful things happen to you."

- Mary Tyler Moore

June 11

"*Most men experience getting older with regret, apprehension. But most women experience it even more painfully: with shame. Aging is a man's destiny, something that must happen because he is a human being. For a woman, aging is not only her destiny... it is also her vulnerability.*"

- Susan Sontag

July 21

"Indecision is fatal.
It is better to make a wrong decision than
build up a habit of indecision."

- Marie Beynon Ray

June 12

"We grew into people that were
not compatible,
I loved him more like a brother."

- Cynthia Baumann

July 20

"The best cosmetic in the world is an active mind that is always finding something new."

- Mary Meek Atkeson

June 13

"If we have not achieved our early dreams, we must either find new ones or see what we can salvage from the old."

— Rosalynn Smith Carter

July 19

"*Don't be afraid your life will end;*
be afraid that it will never begin."

-Grace Hansen

June 14

Flag Day

"One heart, one hope, one destiny,
one flag from sea to sea."

- Kate Brownlee Sherwood

July 18

"*You are unique,
and if that is not fulfilled,
then something has been lost.*"

— *Martha Graham*

June 15

"The true woman is as yet
a dream of the future."

- Elizabeth Cady Stanton

July 17

"*You have a wonderful child. Then, when he's 13, gremlins carry him away and leave in his place a stranger who gives you not a moment's peace. You have to hang in there, because two or three years later, the gremlins will return your child, and he will be wonderful again.*"

— Jill Eikenberry

June 16

"Self-development is a higher duty than self-sacrifice. The thing which most retards and militates against women's self-development is self-sacrifice."

- Eliabeth Cady Stanton

July 16

"I think housework is the reason
most women go to the office."

- Heloise Cruse

June 17

"I think something is only dangerous if you are not prepared for it or if you don't have control over it or if you can't think through how to get yourself out of a problem."

- Judith Resnik

July 15

*"My mother used to say,
'He who angers you, conquers you!'
But my mother was a saint."*

- Elizabeth Kenny

June 18

"I have thought that a woman should be
independent and not regard matrimony as
the only thing to be desired in life."

- Helen Herron Taft

July 14

*"Every child has a right
to a good home."*

-Ettie Lee

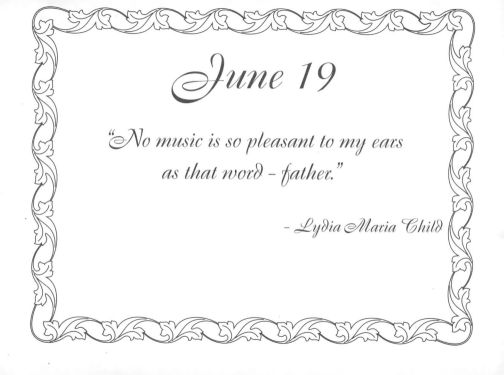

June 19

*"No music is so pleasant to my ears
as that word – father."*

– Lydia Maria Child

July 13

"You've got to get up every morning
with a smile on your face
And show the world all the love in your heart
Then people gonna treat you better
You're gonna find, yes you will,
That you're beautiful as you feel."

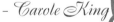
- Carole King

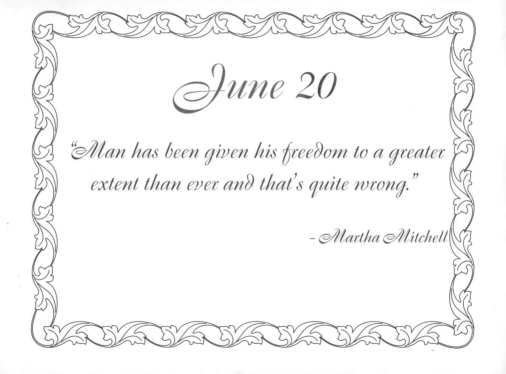

June 20

"Man has been given his freedom to a greater extent than ever and that's quite wrong."

- Martha Mitchell

July 12

"It has long been my belief that in times of great stress, such as a four-day vacation, the thin veneer of family unity wears off almost at once, and we are revealed in our true personalities."

- Shirley Jackson

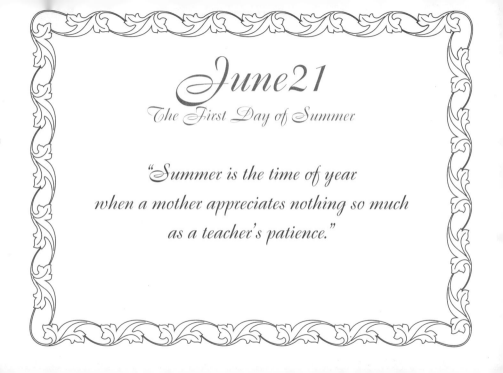

June 21

The First Day of Summer

"Summer is the time of year
when a mother appreciates nothing so much
as a teacher's patience."

July 11

"We were raised with the idea that we had limitless
chances and we got very shocked
to learn that wasn't the case."

- Linda Ronstadt

June 22

Children's Day

"The finest inheritance you can give to a child is to allow it to make its own way, completely on its own feet."

- Isadora Duncan

July 10

"The thing you have to be prepared for is that other people don't always dream your dream."

— Linda Ronstadt

June 23

"When a child enters the world through you,
it alters everything on a psychic, psychological
and purely practical level. You're just not free
anymore to do what you want to do.
And it's not the same again. Ever."

- Jane Fonda

July 9

"Once you've been No. 1,
you can never be satisfied with less."

- Chris Evert Lloyd

June 24

"I am not a do-gooder. I am a revolutionary. A revolutionary woman."

- Jane Fonda

July 8

*"Unless you choose to do great things with it,
it makes no difference how much you are rewarded,
or how much power you have."*

- Oprah Winfrey

June 25

"But the whole point of liberation is that you get out. Restructure your life. Act by yourself."

— Jane Fonda

July 7

"You can have it all.
You just can't have it all at one time."

— Oprah Winfrey

June 26

"...the sudden desire to look beautiful made her straighten her back. Beautiful? For whom? Why, for myself, of course."

— Colette

July 6

*"You cannot love people who refuse
to help themselves."*

- Oprah Winfrey

June 27

"A mother is not a person to lean on but a
person to making leaning unnecessary."

- Dorothy Canfield Fisher

July 5

"I have a lot of things to prove to myself.
One is that I can live my life fearlessly."

- Oprah Winfrey

June 28

"If you do not tell the truth about yourself
you cannot tell it about other people."

-Virginia Woolf

July 4

Independence Day

"One of the fallacies of summer holidays is that you are going to get some serious reading done while you are lying on the beach."

- Nancy Stah

June 29

"*Anything may happen when womanhood has ceased to be a protected occupation.*"

-Virginia Woolf

July 3

"It isn't until you come to a spiritual
understanding of who you are -
not necessarily a religious feeling, but deep down,
the spirit within - that you can begin to take control."

- Oprah Winfrey

June 30

"For most of history,
anonymous was a woman."

— Virginia Woolf

July 2

"*Luck is a matter of preparation meeting opportunity.*"

— Oprah Winfrey

Oprah Winfrey
Born 1954

Fearless, spontaneous, warm, and witty, Oprah is an inspiration to millions. An Emmy award winner, Academy and Golden Globe nominated actress, Oprah dedicates much of her life to helping others less fortunate.

NOV 26

July 1

"Doing the best at this moment puts you in the best place for the next moment."

- Oprah Winfrey